CW00566074

DAVE'S BOOK OF

AUSSIE
SLANG

Published in 2022 by OH! Life
An imprint of Welbeck Non-Fiction Limited, part of Welbeck Publishing Group.
Based in London and Sydney.
www.welbeckpublishing.com

Cover image: Anton Yubran/Shutterstock; Other images courtesy Shutterstock.

A CIP catalogue record for this book is available from the British Library.

ISBN 978-1-83861-129-3

Associate Publisher: Lisa Dyer
Copyeditor: Nicolette Kaponis
Designer: James Pople
Production Controller: Felicity Awdry

Printed and bound in China

10 9 8 7 6 5 4 3 2 1

DAVE'S BOOK OF

★ ★

AUSSIE
SLANG

THE HUMOUR HIDDEN IN A NATION'S CHAT

DAVE ANDREW

CONTENTS

INTRODUCTION

Whether your journey takes you up the road, interstate or across the world, communication with the locals is a hurdle the best travellers know how to jump.

Speaking proper-like in Australia does not mean the Queen's English. Certain words and phrases capture the heart of a place in a way upstanding vowels and consonants cannot.

Slang is the humour-and-metaphor sandwich which makes up the casual speech of a place. This book will have you taking a bite, and enjoying the taste!

Say you have crossed a river, state lines or even the equator to arrive in a wondrous new part of Down

Under. Wouldn't it be great to have an iconic phrase on the tip of your tongue, instead of something that is about as useful as an ashtray on a motorbike?

At first glance, Straya may seem as rough as a pair of hessian undies. However, being equipped with a proper understanding and use of Australian slang – known as Strine – will bring its own rewards.

Instead of Shano saying, 'Catch ya after knock-off' and dropping you at the servo, he might think you are the duck's nuts. Not to piss in your pocket, but fully sick. In which case, you'll be blowing the top off a few frothy ones with a couple of mates in short order.

So, welcome, wherever you are from and wherever you are going.

CHAPTER 1

ORIENTATION

We are going to start at the beginning. Think of this chapter like a compass, a true north to help understand this vast country of powerful nature, extreme beauty and happy-go-lucky people.

GEOGRAPHICAL NOMENCLATURE

Apple Eaters	Residents of Tasmania (Tas). Tasmania used to be one of the largest apple producers in the world. Also, the island looks like an apple.
Cockroaches	Residents of New South Wales (NSW). Humid weather suits the breeding of cockroaches.
Banana Benders/ Cane Toads	Residents of Queensland (QLD). Tropical weather means bananas grow like crazy and venomous cane toads breed like crazy.
Crow Eaters	Residents of South Australia (SA). During the 1800s, times were that tough they ate crows for meat.
Round-a-bouters	Residents of the Australian Capital Territory (ACT). There are many traffic circles used to regulate vehicle flow in Australia's best-planned town.
Cabbage Patchers	Residents of Victoria (Vic). Pejorative term used for the smaller state south of NSW.
Sandgropers	Residents of Western Australia (WA). There's a lot of desert in Straya's remote west.
Top Enders	Residents of the Northern Territory (NT).

CAPITAL CITIES

You hear:	It means:
'Rads', 'Radders', 'Radelaide'	**Adelaide**
'Big Smoke', 'Sin City', 'Emerald City'	**Sydney**
'Melbs', 'Melbum', 'Bleak City'	**Melbourne**
'Not Sydney or Melbourne'	**Canberra**
'Purf', 'Pcity'	**Perth**
'Dtown'	**Darwin**
'The Bart', 'Hobes' or 'Hobie Town'	**Hobart**

UNITS OF DISTANCE

A Bee's Dick   Smallest unit of measure.

Coo-ee   Not within earshot, i.e., not within coo-ee.

Back Blocks   Outer edge of the city.

Whoop Whoop   General term for somewhere too far to travel to.

Back of Bourke   Front of Bourke is already 1,000km from the coast.

Back of Beyond   Beyond is generally accepted as way past Bourke.

Beyond the Black Stump   A mythical object. There are no signposts or phone reception out here. An unimaginable distance.

The Never-never   A vast, uncross-able desert with nothing but horizon in every direction.

HELLOS

G'day	Warm greeting for people you have just met and those you have known all your life.
G'day Mate	A more formal version of the above.
S'garnon?	What is going on?
How's It Hanging?	How is everything with you? (Used by two males.)
Howzit G'arn? Ooright?	How are you going? Alright?
How Ya Travellin'?	How are you?
I Haven't Seen You in Donkey's!	An address to a party you have not seen for a long time.

GOODBYES

Hooroo	Relaxed Aussie goodbye, often accompanied by a wave.
Take It Easy	As stated.
Catch Ya	Catch up with you later.
Cop-u-later	See you soon.
Cheers Mate	Nice to see you.
Choof Off	We better be on our way.

STRINE

Slang is the art of saying something old in a new way. It is often humorous, sometimes indecent and occasionally obscene. Strine is the term for Australian slang, where words are shortened and meanings twisted to come up with something that fits just right, like a pair of budgie smugglers.

TIME

Bush Alarm Clock	Kookaburra's laugh at first light.
Sparrow's Fart	Dawn, i.e., 'I get up at sparrow's fart to go to work.'
In Two Shakes of a Lamb's Tail	Soon.
In a Jiffy	One moment.
Any Tick of the Clock	An event is imminent.
Waiting Till the Cows Come Home	An interminable wait.
Arvo	Afternoon.
Dawnie	Sunrise.
Golden Hour	Sunset.
Evo	Evening.
Call It a Day	To finish up.
Knock-off Time	To finish work.
Broken Hill Time	Someone who is always half an hour late operates on ...
A Month of Sundays	A great distance into the future.

SOCIAL CLASS SYSTEM

Little Aussie Battler A member of the working class, battling to make ends meet.

Colourful Racing Identity A member of the criminal underclass.

Blue Blood Rich snobs.

Dinks Double income, no kids.

Girl's Blouse Timid, uncommitted male.

Karen Irritating, entitled white women behaving badly. A now universal term heard Straya-wide.

Devil Dodger Pious Christian attending more than one weekly church service.

Greenie Environmentalist.

Skip (from *Skippy* the TV show) A term for Australians of British ancestry.

Grey Nomads Retirees towing caravans around Straya.

'A FAIR GO'

This iconic Aussie phrase sums up our core values of justice and fair play and captures Australia's rejection of the pompous English class system. Straya strives to be a country where everybody has an equal opportunity to improve their lot by hard work and aptitude. The widespread acceptance of this attitude can be seen in things like Australia's universal healthcare. At its heart, 'a fair go' is a request for someone to be treated equally and to be given a chance to succeed. This same idea can be expressed with various degrees of playfulness:

A Fair Shake
A Fair Crack of the Whip
A Fair Suck of the Sauce Bottle
A Fair Suck of the Siberian Sandshoe
A Fair Suck of the Raw Prawn

CURRENCY

Avocado	A new, green $100 note.
Green Soldier	A $100 note, which features General John Monash.
Ghost and Bradman	A $100 note. Refers to Don Bradman's 99.94 test cricket batting average.
Jolly Green Giant/ Watermelon/Tree Frog/ Peppermint	A $100 note (green in colour).
Pineapple/Banana	A $50 note (yellow in colour).
Lobster/Red-back	A $20 note (red in colour).
Tenner/Blue Swimmer/ Blue Heeler/Banjo	A $10 note (blue in colour), which features poet, A.B. 'Banjo' Paterson.

Fiver/Sky Diver/ Pink Lady/Prawn	A $5 note (pink in colour), which features Queen Elizabeth II.
Shrapnel	Coins, loose change.
A Brass Razoo	Mythical coin with no value, i.e., 'Not worth a brass razoo!'

ATTIRE

Clobber	Clothes.
Strides	Trousers.
Togs/Cossie/Bathers	Swimsuit.
Daks	Men's pants, short or long.
Trackie Daks	Tracksuit pants.
Flanno	Flannelette shirt.
Jocks	Men's underpants.
Boardies	Men's swimwear.
Budgie Smugglers	Speedo briefs for men.
Dental Floss	String bikini.
Coota Suit	Double denim.

Glad Rags	Your best clothes.
Jumper	Sweater.
Ugg Boots	Sheepskin boots originally worn by airmen to keep warm in the high altitudes during WWI and WWII. Worn by surfers in the 1960s and now used worldwide.
Darwin Pyjamas	No pyjamas (Darwin is very hot and humid).
Hipster Hat	Knitted hat/beanie.
Runners	Trainers/sneakers.
PJs	Pyjamas.

AROUND THE HOUSE

Dunny/Loo	Toilet.
Poo Tickets/Bog Roll/ Date Roll	Toilet paper.
Granny Flat	Self-contained accommodation, either attached to a house or adjacent.
Air-con	Air conditioning.
Brolly	Umbrella.
Doona	A quilted bedspread filled with down or synthetic padding.
Flatmate	A person with whom you share a flat/house.
Light Globe	Light bulb.
Reno	Renovation.
Ute	Pick-up truck.
Torch	Flashlight.
Tip	Garbage dump.
Veranda	Porch.
Ring-stretcher/Treadly	Bicycle.
Workbench	Single man's mattress.
Hills Hoist	Rotary clothes line. Named after its inventor, Lance Hill.

'TRUE BLUE'

In Australia, it is important to be someone genuine, trustworthy and reliable. A real person with no phoney airs and graces. Someone willing to do their share with a smile on their face. These qualities are highly valued and summed up in these catch-all phrases.

If someone says you are:

True Blue,

Dinky-di,

Ridgy-didge

or Fair Dinkum,

take it as a mark of acceptance and a compliment of the highest order.

THINGS ARE GOING WELL

Bewdy	Beautiful.
Bottler	Anything that is its best self.
Rip-snorter	Fabulous.
Ball-tearer	Superb.
Deadly	Excellent/cool/awesome.
She'll Be Right	Affirmation of success.
She'll Be Apples	Everything is going to be OK.
You Beauty	A joyful cry.
Too Right	Absolute alignment of goals.
You Ripper	Tremendous outcome.
Fabbo	Think fabulous with gusto.
You Wouldn't Be Dead for Quids	Lustful appreciation of life in Oz.
Better Than Lego	The feeling of winning a footy Grand Final.

THINGS ARE NOT GOING WELL

Busted	Caught red-handed.
To Cop It Sweet	To endure/take your medicine.
Not Much Chop	Poor-quality situation.
Not My Cup of Tea	Not something you would choose.
Not My Bowl of Rice	Not to my taste.
'Ave a Go Ya Mug!	Exhortation to try harder.
Brain Explosion	Out of character act in the heat of the moment.
Belt Up	Toughen up.
I Need a Cup of Tea, a Bex and a Good Lie Down	Needing a time-out to process whatever just happened.

CHAPTER 2

FOOD & DRINK

In a country as big and hot as Australia, you are bound to need something to eat and a cool beverage to wash it all down. Here is everything you need to maintain bodyweight, quench your thirst and form close personal bonds with your hosts.

HAVING A BEER

Staying hydrated on the world's driest continent makes good sense. But having a drink in Australia is about much more than cooling off. If you are invited for a beer, it is about forming friendships, being accepted and getting to know the community. Once in the pub, though, it is best to know glass sizes before things get out of hand.

BEER GLASS SIZE

Throw Down A small bottle of beer that can be knocked back quickly.

Pony 140ml. Quaint.

Middy/Pot/Handle/Seven 285ml. OK.

Schooner/Pint 425ml. Respectable.

Jug 1.4L. Happy days.

Stubby 375ml. Iconic.

Longneck/Tallie/Big Bot 750ml. Good for benders.

Darwin Stubby 2.25L. World's biggest bottle of beer!

Slab A carton of two dozen. Recognised as a store of value long before Bitcoin. Universal currency stronger than the US dollar.

Stubby Holder Polystyrene-insulated holder to keep a stubby cold.

Dapto Briefcase/Goon 4L cask/box of cheap wine.

DRINKING

Beer O'clock	The minute work finishes.
Roadie	A beer you take with you in the car.
Hair of the Dog	The first beer of the morning after.
Heart Starter	A beer taken early in the day.
Shower Beer	First beer after work, consumed in the shower. Favoured by landscapers.
Two-pot Screamer	A drinker unable to hold their beer.
Grog Horrors	Bad hangover.
Unleaded	Low-strength beer.
Plonk	Cheap wine.
Cardboardeaux	Red wine from cask/box.
Skull/Skol	To drain the entire contents of one's drink in a single draught.
Dead Marine	Empty beer bottle.
On the Wagon	Abstaining from alcohol.
Australian Tai Chi	The act of manoeuvring a large tray of drinks from the bar, through a heaving crowd without excessive spillage.

HITTING
THE TURPS

Australians love 'getting on the grog', 'having a lash' or plainly, having a drink. There are wonderful wineries in every state and territory, a booming craft beer scene and the climate is made for it. It is, therefore, inconceivable you will spend time in Straya and not be offered a glass. When drinking with your new mates, at some stage, you will be expected to shout. Or possibly stand, sneeze, carry the mail, wally grout, wally or bowl. This means buying a round of drinks – the cornerstone of drinking etiquette Down Under.

HUNGER

I Need to Throw on the Nose Bag
Somewhat peckish.

My Stomach Thinks My Throat's Cut
Stomach is grumbling.

I Could Eat an Apple through a Cane Chair
Hungry.

I Could Eat a Horse if You Took Its Shoes Off
Very hungry.

I Could Eat a Horse and Chase Its Rider
Famished.

I Could Eat a Camel's Bum Through a Cane Chair
Dangerously low blood sugar.

I Could Eat the Crotch Out of a Low-flying Duck
Starving.

I Could Eat the Left Leg Off a Skinny Priest
Faint from lack of food.

Chokkas
Full.

As Full as Centrelink on Payday
Filled to the limit.

As Full as a Seaside Dunny on Boxing Day
Filled beyond capacity.

FOOD & DRINK

OZ: we say

USA: they say

OZ: we say	USA: they say
Rocket	Arugula
Capsicum	Bell Pepper
Biscuits	Cookies
Rockmelon	Cantaloupe
Cheddar Cheese	Tasty Cheese
Herbs	'Erbs
Silver Beet	Swiss Chard
Mince Meat	Ground Beef
Sponge Fingers	Ladyfingers
Profiteroles	Cream Puffs
Zooper Doopers	Freezer Pops
Lollies	Candy
Jelly	Jell-O
Bi-carb Soda	Baking Soda
Veggies	Vegetables
Maccas	McDonald's
Cuppa	Cup of Tea
Sanga	Sandwich
Choccy	Chocolate
Tucker	Food
Avo	Avocado
Barbie	Barbeque
Chook	Chicken
Paw Paw	Papaya
Snag	Sausage
Bum Nuts	Eggs
Adam's Ale	Water
Amber Fluid	Beer
Bubbles	Sparkling wine

QUANTITIES

More Than You Can Poke a Stick At	A large number.
Scarce as Hen's Teeth	Very rare.
Six of One, Half a Dozen of the Other	Not much difference either way.
Shitload	A great abundance.
Skerrick	A tiny fragment.

SLANGUAGE

If you were recently arrived Down Under, it was said the best way to sound like a true-blue Aussie was to speak through clenched teeth to stop the blowflies getting in! Australia has some of the richest, liveliest and funniest slanguage, which comes in handy whether you are applying for citizenship or ordering a meal.

CUISINE

A Sparrow's Breakfast	Crumbs to eat, shit, a good look round.
A Dingo's Breakfast	A scratch, a piss, a good look round.
Counter Lunch	Meal served in the Public Bar (hotel).
Caltex Canape	Meal deal from a petrol station, i.e., meat pie plus chocolate milk.
Bachelor's Handbag	Roast chook from a supermarket, purchased by single male.
Mystery Bag/Banger/Snag	Sausage.
Dog's Eye	Meat pie.
Seven Course Meal	Six pack and a meat pie.
Pie Floater	Pie in pea sauce, claimed by Adelaide.
Dead Horse	Tomato sauce.
Dead-eye/One-eyed Sailor	Egg fried in a hole cut in a slice of bread.
Spag Bol	Spaghetti bolognese.

Pavement Sprayer	Late-night kebab.
Mash	Mashed potatoes.
Rat's Coffin	Sausage roll.
Train Smash	Meal thrown together in haste with whatever is available.
Black Doctor	Can of full-strength cola, curing everything from a hangover to the flu.
Schnitty	Chicken schnitzel.
Pavlova	Meringue dessert with cream and fruit, claimed by New Zealand.
Chew and Spew	Cheap and nasty dining experience.
Underground Mutton	Rabbit.
Duck's Dinner	Drinking without eating.
Liquid Lunch	As above.
Flat White	Coffee with heated milk.

GETTING ON IT

Blow in the Bag	Taking a breathalyser test.
Booze Bus	Mobile police breath-testing unit.
Bottle-o	Bottle shop.
BYO	Bring your own.
Cab Sav	Cabernet sauvignon.
Chardy	Chardonnay.
Savvy B	Sauvignon blanc.
Quiet One	A single, slow drink.
Booze Up	Rowdy get-together over many hours.
Getting on It	To concentrate on drinking above all other considerations.
Bender	Consecutive days of solid drinking, food optional.
Shandy	Beer and lemonade mix.
Anzac Shandy	Beer and champagne mix.
Greenie	One can of Victoria Bitter (VB).
Coldy/Frosty/Bevvy	Any beer.
Brownie	Bottle of beer.
Bundy	Rum.
Lolly Water	Soft drink/soda.
Champers	Champagne.
Cleanskin	Wine bottle without label.

SCALE OF INEBRIATION

Gut Full of Piss
Having filled one's stomach to capacity with beer.

Full as a Goog
Having swelled one's stomach with beer into the shape of a soft-boiled egg, otherwise known as a 'googy' egg.

The Wobbly Boot
The stage when the pavement lurches about unevenly.

Blind
Having lost visual perception due to alcohol.

Hammered
Having lost the capacity to anchor oneself in time and space.

Legless
Having lost the capacity to walk.

Trolleyed
Responsibility for physical safety handed over to friends who are moving you by trolley or shopping cart.

Rotten
Having lost ideas of right and wrong.

Smashed
Having surrendered all responsibility.

Blotto
No longer able to see, hear or speak.

Maggoted
You no longer function.

Technicolour Yawn/ Spackle/Chunder/ Spew
To vomit.

CHAPTER 3

SOCIAL SKILLS & DATING

Since the beginning of time, every civilisation has undertaken the quest to find love and popularity. Australia is of course, 'same, same ... but different'. Never fear though, here is all the slanguage you need to thrive romantically and socially Down Under.

ARCHETYPES

Imagine you had just entered a large party and the host was making introductions. After saying their names, they might turn to you muttering under their breath one of the following:

Bludger	Someone with a poor attitude to work.
Dole Bludger	Someone receiving benefits from the government.
Bogan	Unsophisticated, untravelled, uneducated person with loud opinions.
Larrikin	Wild person who has issues with authority figures.
Feral	Conspiracy theorist with aversion to soap.
Sticky-beak	One with a profound interest in other people's business.
Dag	Socially awkward person with a heart of gold.
Whinger	Energy sucker. Complains constantly.
Wouldn't Take Them Fishing	Poor company.
Playing up like a Bali Watch	Mischievous shit-stirrer.
A Loose Unit	Someone who is out of control.
Bible Basher	Religious person who wants to save your soul.

God Botherer	Spiritualist over-concerned with the afterlife.
Tree-hugger	Environmentalist.
Ratbag	Villain.
Yobbo	Uncouth person.
Drongo	Dumb fool/loser.
Wowser	Strait-laced spoilsport puritan.
Wuss	Coward.
Wanker	Idiot.
Vego	Vegetarian.
Wakka	Dickhead/dumb arse.
Clued-up	Smart, wily.
Doesn't Miss a Trick	Intelligent.
Big-noter	Boastful.
Got More Balls Than Keno	Confident and determined. Refers to beloved lottery game.
Bull Artist	Liar.

Stirrer	Troublemaker.
White Shoe Brigade	Property developer.
Battler	Working class.
Bush Baptist	Uncommitted Christian.
Crawler	Servile flatterer.
Dibber Dobber	Tattletale.
Flash as a Rat with a Gold Tooth	Overdressed show-off.
Couch Potato	TV watcher.
Boofhead	Fool.
Dipstick	Buffoon.
Dropkick	Dunce.
Chaos Merchant	Upsetter of apple carts.
Hell-raiser	Crasher of apple carts.
Show Pony	Boastful posturer.
Blow In	Uninvited guest.

EMOTIONAL INTELLIGENCE

Dark on Someone	Not happy with someone.
Bit Aggro	Aggressive.
Frothing at the Mouth	Super-frustrated.
Spitting Chips	Annoyed.
Ropeable	Angry.
Spewing	Very angry.
Pack Your Dacks	Scared.
Packing Death	Very scared.
In the Dumps	Depressed.
In a Lather	Anxious.
Stroppy	Irritable/grumpy.
Happy Little Vegemite	Ecstatic.
Doesn't Know if He's Arthur or Martha	Confused.
Flat as a Tack	Miserable.
Strike Me Pink/Lucky/Purple	Astonished.

Keen as Mustard	Sharply enthusiastic.
As Cross as a Frog in a Sock	Frustrated.
Rooted	Very tired.
To Carry on like a Pork Chop	Behaving in a silly, agitated, excited, unreasonable manner.
You Look like a Stunned Mullet	Surprised.
Up a Gum Tree	Confused.
Cracking a Sad	Dejected.
Nose out of Joint	Irritated.
Chuck a Wobbly	Moment of emotional instability.
Frothing	Bubbly enthusiasm.
If It Was Raining Custard, I'd Only Have a Fork	Self-pity.
Stone the Crows	Amazed.

TAKE CARE

The phrase, 'Life wasn't meant to be easy', was popularised by one of Australia's Prime Ministers. Here are some phrases that mean life has taken someone to a strange place and they are entering the red zone.

Cranky	Annoyed.
Hot under the Collar	Very frustrated.
Throw the Toys out of the Pram	Behave in angry, petulant manner.
Do Your Block	Uncontrollable anger.
Spit the Dummy	Childish, angry outburst.
Blow a Fuse	Explosion of anger.
Do Your 'Nana (Banana)	As above.

LIFE. BE IN IT.

Social gatherings, whether in the backyard,
on the beach or at the sportsground, are
important to life Down Under. For such occasions,
you may be asked to bring an esky (insulated
box to keep drinks cold) with some coldies
(chilled beers) from the bottle-o (liquor store).

SOCIAL INVITATIONS

A Man Is Not a Camel
I need a drink.

Would You like to Bend the Elbow?
Do you fancy a drink?

I'm as Dry as a Dead Dingo's Donger
I'm thirsty, fancy a beer?

I'm Dryer Than a Drover's Dog
Join me for a thirst quencher?

I'm Dryer Than a Pommy's Bathmat
Come, we drink.

I'm Dry as a Kookaburra's Khyber
Emphatic invitation to imbibe.

I Could Murder a Beer
We drink.

I Don't like Drinking on My Pat Malone
Rhyming slang for not wanting to drink alone.

Fancy Cracking a Tinny?
Would you like to open a can of beer?

Wrap Your Laughing Gear around This
Eat/drink this.

As Full as a Seaside Dunny on Boxing Day
Filled beyond capacity.

SOCIAL CUES

Brekkie
First meal of the day/breaking one's fast.

Luncho
After morning tea/before afternoon tea.

Nosh Up
Evening meal.

A Feed
Any of the above.

Chow Time
Time to eat.

Bog In/Dig In
Formal instruction by host to commence a meal.

Bring a Plate
Instruction to guests to bring salad/dessert/meat by host after giving invitation to a social function. Not related to being short of crockery.

Give Someone a Bell
Call someone.

Shoey
Drinking beer out of a shoe to mark a special occasion.

Was Your Father a Glassmaker?
Expression used when someone blocks your view.

Were You Born in a Tent?
Expression used for someone who doesn't close the door behind them.

THE HUMAN BODY

**Wearing One's Birthday Suit/
In the Altogether/In the Nuddy**
Naked.

An Awning over the Toyshop
Male beer belly.

**Apricot/Plums/Jatz Crackers/
Gangoolies/Crown Jewels/
Family Jewels**
Testicles.

Donger/Doodle/Old Fella
Penis.

Date/Ring/Freckle/Quoit
Anus.

Tootsie
Toe.

Pie-hole
Mouth.

Hooter/Bugle/Snoz/Conk
Nose.

Dial
Face.

Mollyducker/Cack-handed
Left-handed person.

**Siphon the Python/Point Percy
at the Porcelain**
Male number one.

Open One's Lunch/Drop Your Guts
Fart.

**Going to See a Man about
a Dog**
Going to the toilet.

**Going to Pinch a Loaf/The
Tortoise Is Poking Its Head Out**
A number two.

Lip Rug
Moustache.

Bum Fluff
Adolescent attempt at growing
facial hair.

Mullet
Hairstyle with short, buzz-cut sides and neck length, or 'party', in the back.

Cul-de-sac
A receding hairline now resembling a dead-end street.

Muffin Top
Belly fat protruding over the front and sides of pants.

Love Handles
Rolls of fat on sides of abdomen big enough to be grasped during lovemaking.

Norks
Women's breasts.

Skinny as a Rake
Thin.

Spent Too Long in the Top Paddock
Plump.

Fat as a Drover's Dog
Thin.

Fat as a Butcher's Pup
Obese.

Short Arse
Of small height.

Plank
Thin and tall.

From Arsehole to Breakfast
From head to toe.

Bolt-ons
Breast implants.

Deaf as a Door Post
Hearing impaired.

Kicked the Bucket/Carked It/ Cashed His Cheque
Dead.

Bag of Donuts
Fat person.

Built like a Brick Shithouse
Strong, muscly human.

Graveyard Chompers
False teeth.

Broad in the Beam
Fat bottom.

Pommy Shower
No water but ample deodorant.

Spit-bath
No bath but wash with flannel.

3Ss
Shit, shower, shave.

INTIMACY

Crack onto Someone
To pursue a person with a view
to romance.

Crack a Fat
Erection.

Map of Tassie
Women's pubis resembling
the shape of Tasmania.

Lip Lock
A kiss.

Pash
A kiss involving tongue.

Up the Duff/Banged Up
Pregnant.

Hickey
Love bite.

A Bun in the Oven
A woman full of child.

Root
The art of the physical union/
consummation. (As a general
rule, Australians do not root for
their favourite team.)

Cut Your Lunch
When someone moves in on
your love interest.

Give Someone the Flick
Breaking off the relationship.

Horizontal Folk Dancing
See Root.

Feeling Clucky
Ready for children.

On the Swipes
The search for love over Wi-Fi.

Toey as a Roman Sandal
Feeling amorous.

Root Rat
Someone constantly looking for sex.

Dunlop Overcoat/Franger
Condom.

To Throw a Leg Over
Sexual intercourse.

Get Your Rocks Off
Male orgasm.

Wombat
Somebody who eats, roots, shoots and leaves.

Wristy
The act of giving manual stimulation.

Vatican Roulette
Rhythm method of contraception.

Frigid Digit
Erectile dysfunction.

To Have Had Your Beer Goggles On
To have woken up with someone who looked more attractive the night before.

Get off at Redfern
The art of coitus interruptus (Redfern is the last stop before arriving at Central Station).

First Base
French kiss.

Jelly Kiss
Kiss given on the labia.

Columbian Kiss
French kiss that involves groping the arse.

Aussie Kiss
French kiss given 'down under'.

German Kiss
French kiss with less tongue.

Dutch Kiss
French kiss with less tongue and more phlegm.

BEAUTY & THE BEAST

Bit of All Right	Attractive.
You Scrub up Nicely	Compliment regarding appearance.
Good Sort	Great girl or decent chap.
Fell out of the Ugly Tree	Ugly.
Having a Face like a Half-sucked Mango	Ugly.
Having a Face like a Dropped Pie	Ugly.
Having a Face like a Burnt Thong	Ugly.
Having a Face like a Half-chewed Minty	Ugly.
A Face Only a Mother Could Love	Frightful.
Fugly	Offensive to the sight.
Ugly as a Hatful of Arseholes	Terrifically unfortunate in life's lottery.

FAMILY RELATIONS

Bloke	Man.
Sheila/Skirt	Woman.
Ankle Biter/Little Tacker	Child.
Oldies	Parents.
Hubby	Husband.
Missus	Wife.
Skin and Blister	Sister.
Battle Axe	Mother-in-law.
Bomb Thrower	Wife/girlfriend.
Trouble and Strife	Wife.
Better Half	Term used by men for their partner in rare moments of self-appraisal.
Relo	Relative.
Old Fossil	Geriatric in wisdom years.

CHAPTER 4

INDUSTRIAL RELATIONS

Australians share a complex relationship with work. With stunning beaches, coral reefs, walking trails and so much sunshine, it's a wonder anything gets done at all. However, thriving cities and productive farms are testament to the blood, sweat and tears of generations. When pushed, Aussies can dig in. Here is the slanguage you need to understand the most complicated of workplace environs.

PROFESSIONS

Postie	Postal worker.
Milko	Milkman.
Journo	Journalist.
Pollie	Politician.
Garbo/Garbologist	Garbage person.
Tradie	Coverall term for tradesperson.
Brickie	Bricklayer.
Sparkie	Electrician.
Chalkie	Teacher.
Truckie	Truck/semi/tractor trailer driver.
Pumpie	Someone who pours concrete on job sites.
Chippie	Carpenter.
Doc/Quack	Doctor.
Cabbie	Taxi driver.
Muso	Coverall term for musician.

Fiery	Firefighter.
Ambo	Ambulance driver (and the ambulance itself).
Copper/Pigs/Boys in Blue	Police officer.
Nipper	Young surf lifesaver.
Suit	Professional office worker.
Bean Counter	Accountant.
Cut Lunch Commando	Army reserve person.
Grey Ghost/Brown Bomber	Parking inspector.
Sparrow Starver	Street sweeper.
Fisho	Fishmonger.
Gyno	Gynaecologist.
Paper Shuffler	Office administrator.

HARD YAKKA (WORK)

To let you know an honest day's labour has been done,
Australians might tell you they have been:

Flat Out	No time to play.
Flat Chat	No time to talk.
Flat to the Boards	Going as fast as I can.
Flat Out like a Lizard Drinking	Arrived early, left late.
Flat Out like a One-armed Bricklayer in Baghdad	Literally did not stop all day.
Flat Out like a One-armed Bill Poster on a Windy Day	Tremendous effort.
Flat Out like a Maggot on a Chop	Obsessive work ethic.
Busy as a One-legged Bloke in an Arse-kicking Contest	Zen-like focus.
Busy as a Centipede on a Hot Plate	Hyperactive.

TALL POPPY SYNDROME

This syndrome is a social phenomenon that occurs in Australia where people criticise those who have achieved great success. It is the downside of egalitarian ideals and hinges around the expectation that poppies should grow to a uniform height. It means criticism of anyone rising above the station of the common person. At its worst it can celebrate the downfall of someone different, successful or eccentric.

COLLEAGUES

The Australian workplace is as diverse as the country, made up of long-haul truck drivers to sheep shearers, barrier reef tour guides to shawarma purveyors, office workers to farmers and everything in-between. No matter the workplace, chances are you will recognise some of these characters.

Sensor Light	Only works if someone is walking past.
Noodles	Thinks all jobs take two minutes.
The Blister	Appears when the hard work is done.
The Lantern	Not very bright and has to be carried.
Harvey Norman	Been there three years with no interest.
Deckchair	Always folds under pressure.
Perth	Three hours behind everyone else.
G-spot	Can never be found.
Bushranger	Holds everyone up.
Wheelbarrow	Only works when pushed.
The Limo	Carries eight people.
Cordless	Charges all night but only works for two hours.
Drill Bit	A small, boring tool.
Sniper's Nightmare	Worker with one short and one long leg causing him to bob.

BUSINESS TERMINOLOGY

Go down the Gurgler
Total failure of enterprise.

Go like Hot Cakes
Selling very quickly.

Deep Pockets
Person with money that doesn't spend it.

Hip-pocket Nerve
Wallet/bank account.

Big Bickies
Large sum of money.

Bottom-of-the-harbour Scheme
Tax avoidance by smart accountant.

Cook the Books
Unreliable ledger.

Pull Your Socks Up
Try harder/lift your game.

Put Your Head Down
Concentrate to the exclusion of all else.

Rough End of the Pineapple
Poor end of the deal.

Two-bobs' Worth
An opinion.

Put in the Hard Yards
Working hard to achieve your goal.

Right as Rain
Our agreement holds.

Sink the Fangs
Acute, desperate request for a loan.

Got You by the Short and Curlies
Bargaining position with poor leverage.

Got You by the Balls
Bargaining position with zero leverage.

Got Legs
Idea with a good chance of succeeding.

Get the Nod
Application approved.

Sling/Backhander
Bribe.

Smoko
Short, informal break from work
(cigarette optional).

Bite Merchant
Persistent borrower.

Compo
Worker's compensation.

Arse Kisser
A person who flatters to
gain favour.

Corporate Fluffer
A person who excels by
kissing arse.

Captain's Pick
Inept, autocratic decision
favoured by team leaders.

Rort
Illegal racket.

Nut Out
Figure out an agreement.

Mates Rates
Discount for friends.

Moolah
Money.

Offsider
Helper.

Good Oil
Quality insider information.

Doing a Runner
To escape without paying
a debt.

To Be Dudded
Sold something that was
not authentic.

To Be Fleeced
To be cheated.

Taken to the Cleaners
To be swindled out of
everything.

Belly Up
Insolvent/bust.

Bright Spark
Smart person.

ECONOMY

Whether at the races, the bar or the bank manager's office, money matters require clear communication.

I'm Strapped	Low on cash.
Broke	No money at all.
Fast Women and Slow Horses	Broke.
Short Arms, Long Pockets	Someone who is not generous with their money.
Taken to the Cleaners	Lost everything.
What Do You Do for a Crust?	What is your occupation?
What's the Damage?	How much does it cost?
Your Cheque Is in the Mail	Stop worrying, you will get paid.

Cheque in the Boot	To be fired from work without words being exchanged.
Put It on the Never-never	Paying for something on credit.
Pay through the Nose	An exorbitant amount.
More Bang for Your Buck	Something of better value.
Flogging the Plastic	Overuse of a credit card.
Whip-around	Impromptu collection for someone in dire need.
Champagne Lifestyle on a Beer Budget	Spending more than you earn.

CHAPTER 5

CULTURAL INSIGHTS

Earth's largest island? A continent? Either way, Australians are proud of their country and in thrall to its magnificent landscape. The smell of the bush, the colour of the light, the calls of the animals and the richness of the soils are all unique. Australia is also a melting pot of different cultures. It is little wonder, then, that you will encounter some choice phrases. Here is a friendly hand to help you get a grip on things.

ROO STEAKS

The kangaroo is unique to Australia and one of its national symbols. The kangaroo adorns currency, stamps and the coat of arms. It may, then, come as a surprise to also find kangaroo on the menu! Roo steaks and roo sausages, known as 'kanga bangers', are rich in iron and can be found in most butchers and supermarkets. Delicious!

FAUNA RELATED

Shark Bait	The person farthest out to sea in a pack of swimmers.
Snake	Someone who cannot be trusted.
Big Hat, No Cattle	Someone unable to back up their words with actions.
Squirrel Grip	A tackle where pressure is applied to the testicles.
Like a Rat up a Drainpipe	Instinctually taking advantage of a situation.
A Dog's Breakfast	Disorganised situation.
Barmy as a Bandicoot	Mad.
Bald as a Bandicoot	Completely bald.
Acting the Goat	Behaving badly.
Mad as a Cut Snake	Angry/disturbed.
Make a Galah of Yourself	A fool.
Pack of Galahs	No-hopers.
Pig's Arse	I don't think so.
Stone the Crows	I can't believe it.
Get up My Goat	Getting on my nerves.
Rabbits On	Talks nonsense.
Wombat	Slow/lazy.

FIRST AID

Poorly
Hungover/relationship difficulty/ common cold.

Feeling a Bit Crook
Unwell and requiring a legitimate day off work.

Green around the Gills
Acute sickness.

Sick as a Dog
Umbrella term used to describe hangovers/stomach upsets/flu.

Crook as Rookwood
Serious illness named after Rookwood, a large cemetery in Sydney.

Chucking a Sickie
To take the day off work while in perfect health. Known to occur when surf is good.

'USELESS'

'Useless' is a coverall phrase describing incompetence and often used for politicians and their sons. It can be teamed with metaphors for added emphasis:

Useless as Tits on a Bull

Useless as a Screen Door on a Submarine

Useless as a Chocolate Teapot

Useless as an Ashtray on a Motorbike

Useless as a Glass Door on a Dunny (Toilet)

Useless as a Roo Bar on a Skateboard

'NO WORRIES'

Australia is a big country – the world's sixth largest –
where communities are tested by fires, droughts
and floods. Living here means getting over these
challenges with a helping hand from your mates.
'No worries' is an iconic Aussie phrase that means
'It will all be OK', or 'You're welcome, mate,' because
we are all in this together.

FROM THE HEART OF
THE AUSSIE PSYCHE

Cheeky Little Possum
Incorrigibly naughty, but loveable person.

Chuck a U-E
To turn around and head back to where you came.

Like Flies round the Dunny Door
Rapidly growing crowd of people.

Cop a Load of That
Look at that!

Better Than a Poke in the Eye with a Blunt Stick
See, things are not as bad as you think.

Panic Merchant
A person who immediately thinks the worst.

He Could Talk under Wet Cement
Someone who loves a yarn.

Not Enough Brains to Give Himself a Headache
As stated.

Drinking with the Flies
Drinking alone, aka a horrid state of affairs.

You've Got Two Chances, Buckley's and None
Zero chance what you want will happen.

Anne's Your Aunty
And there you have it.

Bob's Your Uncle
Success is guaranteed.

Have a Lend Of
To take advantage of someone.

Turn-up for the Books
A surprise result.

Happy Little Vegemite
A contented child.

ADD AN 'O'

Cutting things down to size is embedded in the Australian psyche. If you get too big for your boots, your mates will cut you down to size. The same goes for language. Don't be confused by the endless abbreviations. Simply take the first syllable, cut down the rest and add 'o'.

Aggro	Aggressive.
Compo	Compensation.
Defo	Definitely.
Devo	Devastated.
Salvos	Salvation Army.
Typo	Typing error.
Rego	Vehicle registration

Once you have mastered 'o', you can advance to adding -ie and -y.

Chrissie	Christmas.
Exy	Expensive.
Mushie	Mushroom.
Sunnies	Sunglasses.
Pozzy	Position.
Pressie	Present.
Lippy	Lipstick.

CHAPTER 6

SPORT & LEISURE

Aussies love their sport. Some even believe we are obsessed with it. For a small nation, we punch above our weight when it comes to bats, balls, playing fields, snowfields and oceans. Little wonder, considering our superb climate and wide-open space. Read on to discover idioms that will come in handy when you cross the white line.

BUSHIES, COCKIES, CITY SLICKERS & BEACH BUMS

Despite the stereotype of the Australian Farmer (cockies), or the Rugged Bush Dweller (bushies), over 10 million Australians are city slickers, residing in Sydney or Melbourne. The majority of Australians live within 50km of the coast. Some indeed are surfies and beach bums, enjoying the ocean waves year-round.

SURF

Huey
God who provides swells to surfers.

Slip, Slop, Slap
Exhortation to apply sunscreen. (While Australia is the skin cancer capital of the world, it also leads in treatment.)

The Green Room
Ocean.

Ankle Busters
Small, difficult waves.

Barney
Rookie surfer.

Clam Dragger
Female body boarder.

Dawn Patrol
Early morning surf.

Hang Eleven
Male surfing nude.

Men in Grey Suits
Sharks.

Rip
Strong current away from shore.

Rail Bang
Getting hit between the legs by a surfboard.

Namer
Surfer who overshares locations of the best surf breaks.

Bombie
Offshore reef with surf.

Dumper
Wave that deposits rider onto sand.

Bondi Cigar
Number two in the water.

Brown-eyed Mullet
As above.

CARS

In a country that is 7,692,024km^2, at some stage you are going to need wheels. Here are some words to get you started and make sure you get to where you're going.

100 Clicks	100km.
Juice	Petrol.
Rubber	Tyres.
Spanner Monkey	Mechanic.
Bog/Bondo	Putty filler.
Skid Lid	Helmet.
Anchors	Brakes, i.e., hit the anchors.
Loud Pedal	Accelerator.
Speedo	Speedometer.
Blinkers	Indicator lights.

Tiller	Steering wheel.
Donk	Car engine.
Carby	Carburettor.
End Can	Exhaust.
Ding	Dent.
Roo Bar/Cow Catcher	Fender.
Fang	To drive fast.
Slicks	Tread-less racing tyres.
Pop the Bonnet	Lift the hood.

Run a Red To drive straight through a red light.

Burnout Spinning tyres while standing still.

Circle Work Circular burnouts.

Donut Burning rubber in circles on the road.

Hoon Wild, high-risk driver.

Slammed Vehicle that has been lowered.

Love Tap Minor crash.

Kiss His Arse To hit another car in the rear.

Crotch Rocket Dangerous motorbike.

Shopping Trolley Small-engine hatch.

Bomb Worthless old car.

Yank Tank Car made in the USA.

Toorak Tractor SUV that never ventures off-road.

Rag Top Convertible.

Temporary Australian Motorbike driver.

Bog Standard Basic model.

Slush Box	Automatic transmission.
Four Bangers	Four-cylinder engine.
Six Bangers	Six-cylinder engine.
Sleeper	Standard-looking vehicle with performance engine.
Blown/Boosted	Supercharged.
Launch	Car accelerating from standing start.
Put the Pedal to the Metal	Exhortation to drive faster.
Grip	Tyre's ability to hold the road.
Hairdryer	Police radar gun.
Clocked	Caught on speed camera.
Prang/Stack/Bingle/ Come a Gutser	To have an accident.
The Ton	Going 100kmph.
Blown	Souped-up engine/ exploded engine.
Bush Bash	To go off-road.
That'll Buff Right Out	Sarcastic observation of major damage to vehicle.

SPORTS

Roundball	The World Game/soccer.
Footy	Catchall term for Rugby League, Rugby Union, soccer and Aussie Rules (AFL).
Aerial Ping Pong	Aussie Rules.
Thugby Union/Rah-rah Bum Sniffing	Rugby Union.
Cross-country Wrestling	Rugby League.
Pill	The ball in any footy code.
Throwball	Disrespectful term for Rugby League and Rugby Union.
Behind	Single point score for kicking the ball beside the main goal in Aussie Rules.
Shirtfront	A fierce tackle given chest-to-chest.

Barrack	To cheer for your team.
Biff/Boilover/Stink/ Argie-bargy/Melee	A brawl on the field with, 'melee' being specific to Aussie Rules.
Mongrel Punt	Poor kick.
Early Shower	Player sent from the field for indiscretion.
Backchat	When a player argues with the umpire's decision.
Creamed	When a player or team is beaten badly.
Drown Some Worms	To go fishing.
I Have Caught Australia	A snagged fishing line.

'DOWN THE ROAD'

Combine Australia's great distances, the casual nature of Aussies and their instinct for understatement and 'down the road' becomes a recipe for disaster. This often-used phrase could quite easily mean at the end of the street or 1,000km away. Take care!

THE BUSH

Road Trip	Long driving expedition to the far reaches.
Bush	Anywhere that is not the city.
Bush Telly	Campfire.
Bushranger	Outlaw.
Bushie	Resident of the bush.
Bush Pig	Ugly person.
Bush Quack	Uncertified first-aider.
Bush Lawyer	Unqualified, over-opinionated person.
Bushfire Blonde	Red-haired woman.
Bushman's Hanky	Wiping nose on forearm or blowing out of one nostril.

Station A big farm, e.g., Anna Station in SA which is 23,677km².

Roughing It Camping without luxuries, think boy's weekend.

Glamping Camping with luxuries, think away with the missus.

Bindy Prickle in the grass.

Bush Telegraph Word-of-mouth.

Tinder	Fire kindling (not swiping right).
Billy	Campfire kettle.
Bush Tucker	Native outback food.
Damper	Bread made with flour and water and cooked in coals or a camp oven.
Swag	Roll-up canvas bed.
Long Drop	Toilet over a large hole.
Thunderbox	Outback toilet.
Mozzie	Mosquito.
Brumby	Wild horse.
Paddock Basher	Non-registered off-road vehicle.
Fartsack	Sleeping bag.

ROAD TRIP

A road trip in Australia might mean driving nine hours between Sydney and Melbourne, or crossing deserts where the population is measured by decimal point of persons per 100,000km^2. Therefore, it's good to have your car filled with fuel and drinking water, and good to know with whom you are sharing the road.

Single	A truck towing a single trailer.
B Double	A truck towing a small trailer and a large trailer.
Road Train	A truck towing up to four large trailers with combined weight of over 140 tonnes.
Roller	Rolls-Royce.
Duke	Ducati.
Vee Dub	Volkswagen.
Beamer	BMW.
Commode/Dunny Door/Bomb-a-dore	Commodore.

Bitsaremissing	Mitsubishi.
Hardly Driveable	Harley-Davidson.
Henry	Ford.
Kwaka	Kawasaki.
Pug	Peugeot.
Landy	Land Cruiser.
Tojo	Japanese four-wheel drive.
Mud Plugger	Stripped-down, large-tyred off-roader.
Disco	Land Rover Discovery.
Oil Burner	A diesel vehicle.
Sunday Driver	Slow, unskilled driver.
Revhead	Motoring enthusiast.
Backseat Driver	Passenger issuing instructions to driver.
Human Handbrake	Passenger afraid of speed.
Road Rage	Frustrated and angry driver navigating aggressively.
Off the Beaten Track	Not the road most travelled.
The Scenic Route	Not lost but gone the long way round. Could be lost.

GAMBLING

The story goes Australians will bet on two flies going up a wall. Aussies love a flutter and will place a bet on any of the football codes, a cricket match, tennis game, horse race, hockey match or motorsport race. Also camels, greyhounds, emus, tuna tossing, dunny racing, nude tug-of-war, boat racing in dry riverbeds, gumboot throwing, crab racing, cow racing, cane toad racing ... you get the idea. Here is some slanguage to help you pick a winner.

Have a Flutter	Making a bet, usually for a small amount.
Four-legged Lottery	Horseracing.
The Dogs/Dish Lickers	Greyhound racing.
Pokies/Fruit Machine	Poker machine.
Scratchy	Scratch-and-win lottery ticket.
Furphy	Improbable, false or unreliable rumour.
Wager	A bet.
Punter	Gambler.
Asparagus	Punter who fancies himself as having lots of insider knowledge, i.e., more tips than a can of asparagus.
Grapevine	Universal term for hearsay/gossip heard throughout Straya.
Bolter	Horse/dog/fly at long odds.
Stone Motherless	Finishes last by a huge distance.
Write Your Own Ticket	Your pick is so unlikely to win that the bookmaker is willing to let you set the odds.
Glue on the Shoe	Slow horse.

Grew Another Leg   Sudden improvement in performance.

Late Mail   Last minute information on track, scratching, weather, etc.

Moral   Utter certainty of a win.

Plunge   Rush of money bet on one racer.

Ring In   Animal illegally substituted for another.

Dead Cert   A sure thing.

THE GREAT AUSTRALIAN SALUTE

You see it at the sportsground. In the backyard. At a barbie. Politicians do it. Bricklayers do it. Children do it. If you've lived through an Aussie summer, chances are you, too, have mastered this essential survival skill. It refers to the almost unconscious waving of the hand across the face to brush away the flies.

CHAPTER 7

MUST-HAVES

Australians are a resourceful lot, discovering creative solutions for major problems. Did you know we have Aussies to thank for: black box flight recorders, the electric drill, the winged keel, Wi-Fi, plastic bank notes, one-day cricket and many other useful inventions. They have done it with the language too, high-tackling the Queen's English, face-slapping syllables, shirt-fronting consonants and gut-punching words into fresh combinations which get the job done Down Under.

HAVE

Have a Go	Put your back into it.
Have a Crack	Give it a go.
Have a Lash	Give something a shot.
Have a Burl	To make an attempt.
Have a Bo-Peep	To look.
Have a Heart	To show compassion.
Have a Lend of	To take advantage of a situation or person.
Have a Naughty	Sex.
Have It Off	Sex.
Have a Shot	To verbally attack someone.
Have to Run around in the Shower to Get Wet	A thin person.
Having a Bad Trot	A string of bad luck.
Have a Great Face ` for Radio	Unattractive.
Have Tickets on Yourself	Inflated sense of self.

HASN'T

Hasn't Got a Bean	Broke.
Hasn't Got a Hope	Doesn't have a chance.
Hasn't Got Two Bob to Rub Together	To have no money, not even coins.
Hasn't Got a Clue	Not seeing what is about to happen.
Hasn't Got a Snowball's Chance in Hell	Zero likelihood of success.

RUN

Run In	Disagreement.
Run out of Legs	Exhausted.
Run around like a Chook with Your Head Cut Off	To run fast but get nowhere.
Runs on the Board	Good track record.
The Runs	Diarrhoea.
Run Rings Around	To be faster, smarter and better than others.
Run of Outs	String of defeats.
Run like a Hairy Goat	To run a poor race.

OFF

Off Your Face	Having achieved an elevated plane through the responsible use of alcohol.
Off Your Tits	As above.
Off Your Trolley	As above.
Off Your Chops	As above.
Off Your Tucker	Not hungry.
Off like a Bride's Nightie	Taken off with great speed.
Off the Rails	To be headed for trouble.
Off with the Fairies	Absentminded/preoccupied.
Off like a Bucket of Prawns in the Hot Sun	Strong feeling something is not right.

RIGHT

Righto	OK.
Right On	Emphatic agreement.
Right as Rain	Everything is good.
She'll Be Right	Optimistic projection of outcome.
That Can't Be Right	Expression of surprise, i.e., wife of inveterate gambler getting letter of eviction.
That'd Be Right	Accepting a bad outcome as inevitable, i.e., wife of inveterate gambler hearing he put their rent on a 100 to 1 shot in race 7, 'Yeah, that'd be right.'

FULL

Full   Pissed.

Full On   Intense.

Full of Beans   Energetic.

Fully Sick   Expression of approval/admiration.

Full of It   Pathological liar.

Full as a Boot   Pissed.

ALL

All Froth and No Beer	A person with no depth of character.
All Dressed up with Nowhere to Go	Your date hasn't shown up/the event has been cancelled/there was a misunderstanding about the start time.
All the Go	Something trending with the public.
All over the Place like a Dog's Breakfast	State of disarray/confusion.
All over Red Rover	Utterly finished/at an end.
All Your Christmases Have Come at Once	Remarkable stroke of good fortune.
All Shine and No Shoes	Not genuine and without substance.
All Ears	An attentive listener.
All Smiles	Contented and cheerful.
All Piss and Vinegar	A sour and bitter personality.

GO

Go for Your Life	Not just permission but enthusiastic endorsement.
Go Bush	To leave one's city address for the regional interior.
Go Walkabout	Wandering on a soul's quest without a destination.
Go to Billy Oh	An emphatic request to leave.
Go to Buggery	A more emphatic request to leave.
Go to Hell	As stated.

ON

On a Good Wicket	A favourable situation/well-paid job.
On a Sticky Wicket	Difficult circumstances.
On the Blink	Not working, often to do with the TV.
On the Nose	The suspicion that something is not right.
On the Ball	Punctual, smart and responsible person.
On Your Game	Playing well.
On the Outer	No longer included.
On the Turps	Serious application to the drinking of alcohol.
On the Knocker	Have a perfect understanding.
On the Wrong Track	Heading for trouble.
Onya	Good on you!

DO/DON'T

Do Your Lolly/'Nana   To lose your shit.

Do Your Dough   To lose money.

Do the Dirty   To betray someone.

Do the Harold   To vanish without a trace. Refers to the disappearance of Prime Minister Harold Holt.

Do the Bolt   To run away at high speed.

Do Your Dash   Had your chance.

Do the Trick   This will work.

Don't Come the Raw Prawn with Me   Don't attempt to deceive me.

Don't Get Your Knickers in a Knot   Don't worry about it.

Don't Stick Your Nose In   Don't interfere.

Don't Strain Yourself   Sarcastic encouragement to work harder.

Don't Get off Your Bike   Friendly advice to calm down.

Don't Piss on My Back and Tell Me It's Raining   A failed attempt at deception.

Don't Fret Your Freckle   Don't be anxious.

Don't Pick Your Nose or Your Head Will Cave In   Saying someone is without brains.

GET

Get on Your Bike	Instruction to leave immediately.
Get the Axe	To be sacked from your job.
Get Your Arse into Gear	Exhortation to move faster.
Get Real	Be sensible.
Get on like a House on Fire	To have a natural friendship/ connection.
Get on Your Goat	A state of irritation and annoyance.
Get Nowhere Fast	Working hard with no result.
Get Rinsed	To become intoxicated with alcohol.
Get the Drift	To comprehend.
Get the Guernsey	To be selected.

TAKE

To Take a Piece out Of	To hurt someone.
To Take a Punt	To have a try.
To Take a Shine To	To take a liking to.
Take a Squiz	To have a closer look.
Take the Bull by the Horns	To be proactive.

YOU

You Look like Something the Cat Dragged In	Unkempt, bedraggled appearance.
You Are off the Rails	No longer behaving properly.
You Are Yanking My Chain	Stirring the pot.
You're a Gunna	Someone who talks but never does.
Your Blood's Worth Bottling	A compliment/appreciation of your effort.
Your Goose Is Cooked	To be finished/found out.
You've Got to Be in It to Win It	Exhortation to participate.

GOOD/BAD

Gas Bagger	Good speaker
Got the Gift of the Gab	As above.
Could Talk the Leg off a Table	As above.
Could Talk Underwater	As above.
Could Talk through Wet Cement	As above.
Couldn't Open His Mouth for All the Tea in China	Poor speaker.
Couldn't Speak if His Life Depended on It	Poor speaker.
Built like a Brick Shithouse	Good physical specimen.
Fit as a Mallee Bull	As above.
Bent up like a Half-shut Pocket Knife	Poor physical specimen.

IS/IS NOT

Thong IS a flip-flop
NOT a G-string.

Bird IS a woman
NOT something with feathers.

Rubber IS an eraser
NOT a condom.

Chips ARE French fries
NOT potato crisps.

Bonnet IS the hood of a car
NOT an old-fashioned hat.

The trunk IS the boot of a car
NOT travel luggage.

Crook IS both a criminal and not feeling well.

Chemist IS a pharmacy
NOT a scientist.

Pissed IS being drunk
NOT being angry.

Trolley IS a shopping cart
NOT public transport.

Lemonade IS 7 Up
NOT homemade lemon juice mixed with sugar.

Poppers
are NOT juice boxes ...

WEATHER-ISMS

On an island as big as Australia, with its deserts and rainforests, beaches and mountain ranges, cities and farms, the weather is constantly changing. It's the first subject of conversation among farmers and travellers, surfers and truckies, neighbours and ... everyone, really. Little wonder it's made its way into the idiom.

As Slow as a Wet Week	Every minute feels like an hour.
It's so Windy It Could Blow a Blue Dog off a Chain	Don't put the washing out or wear a hat.
It's that Dry They Had to Close Two Lanes of the Local Pool	Water restrictions apply.
It's so Dry the Trees Are Chasing the Dogs	A bad drought.
It's Hotter than a Shearer's Armpit	Over 45 degrees ... or feels like it.
It's so Windy It Will Blow the Milk out of Your Tea	Don't attempt to put up an umbrella.
It's so Wet It Would Bog a Duck in Boots	Under no circumstances take the car off the bitumen.
It's so Cold It Would Freeze the Balls off a Brass Monkey	You're going to need an extra jumper.

NAMES

In like Flynn	Meaning a certainty of success with a woman. Refers to Australian-born actor, Errol Flynn, who had a penchant for female company.
Joe Bloggs	The average man on the street.
Jack Of	To be fed up with something.
Joey	Baby kangaroo still in its mother's pouch.
One for Ron	Saving something for later.
Happy as Larry	Ecstatic.
Fred Nerk	Cousin of Joe Bloggs.
Bruce	Generic name for a bloke.
Bradbury	Against-the-odds win achieved on the biggest stage. Refers to Steve Bradbury at the 2002 Winter Olympics who won gold after passing six skaters who fell on the final bend.

EITHER/ORS

Billy Either a pot for boiling water or a bong.

Tinny Either a 375ml can of beer or a small boat with an outboard motor.

Thong Either summer footwear or a bikini bottom.

White Pointers Either topless (female) sunbathers or the world's most dangerous shark.

Going Off Either a great party or someone losing their temper.

Lemon Either a machine that is faulty or a piece of fruit.

Hottie Either a hot water bottle or a good-looking person.

Knock Back Either to drink quickly or to refuse someone's amorous advances.

Knock Either to criticise or to tap lightly.

RHYMING SLANG

Rhyming slang originated in London's
East End during the 1800s and the underworld of
America's West Coast. Aussies took the cockney game
and adapted it to suit the conditions Down Under.

Captain Cook	A quick look.
Barry Crocker	To have a shocker (poor performance).
Joe Blake	Snake.
John Dory	Story.
Noah's Ark	Shark.
Skyrocket	Pocket.
China Plate	Mate.
Ned Kelly	Belly.
Polly Waffle	Brothel.
Wally Grout	Shout.
Gary Ablett	Tablet.
Ginger Meggs	Legs.
Warwick Farm	Arm.
Harold Holt	Run away.

Johnny Raper	Paper.
Mal Meninga	Finger.
Paul Keating	Meeting.
Rod Laver	Favour.
Pat Malone	Alone.
Steak and Kidney	Sydney.
Dunlop Tyre	Liar.
Fairy Bower	Shower.
Britney Spears	Beers.
Dalai Lamas	Dramas.

ALL THE REST

Blind Leading the Blind	Two people doing a task neither has any idea about.
Boots 'n' All	Wholeheartedly.
Call a Spade a Spade	To tell it like it is.
Call a Spade a Shovel	Injudiciously heartless delivery of the truth.
Take a Walk in the Hall of Mirrors	Invitation to take a long, hard look at oneself.
Five-finger Discount	Stolen goods.
Go for Broke	To try really hard.
Ball's Up	Mistake/chaos/confusion.
Barking up the Wrong Tree	You are mistaken.
In the Bag	As good as accomplished.
It's Gone Walkabout	To have lost something.
Every Man and His Dog	Everybody.

CHAPTER 8

IMPOLITE TALK

A generous and good-hearted Australian insult can be heard from the kitchen table to Parliament House. If you put an ear to the wall and listen, you'll hear all the things you wanna say, you shouldn't say and some you can't say.

CHARACTER APPRAISAL

As Sharp as a Bowling Ball	Stupid.
As Thick as a Brick	Stupid.
Wouldn't Know if His Arse Was on Fire	Stupid.
Nothing Between the Ears	Empty-headed.
Only Has One Oar in the Water	Daydreamer.
The Light's on But No One's Home	Vacant/vacuous.
The Lift Doesn't Go to the Top Floor	Incapable of advanced reasoning.
Not the Sharpest Knife in the Drawer/ Tool in the Shed	Blunt thinker.

Not the Full Quid	Mentally deficient.
Not Playing with the Full Deck	As above.
A Stubby Short of a Six Pack	Not all there.
A Sandwich Short of a Picnic	As above.
Has a Few Palings Missing from the Fence	Unreliable narrator.
A Few Kangaroos Loose in the Top Paddock	A bit nutty.

INSULTS

Froot Loop	Mad.
Wanker	Self-indulgent/annoyingly pretentious.
Dipstick/Drongo/Dropkick	Fool.
Tickets on Yourself	Prideful overconfidence.
Up Yourself	As above.
Thinks the Sun Shines Out of His Arse	Prone to self-exultation.
Waste of Space	Useless.
Salad Dodger	Obese person.
Screw-up	A blunderer.
Tight as a Fish's Arse	Not inclined to shout beers.
Slack-arse	A lazy person.
Straighty	Conservative/no fun.
A Waste of Space	Dumb/useless.
Muppet	Stupid.
Fuck-knuckle	Stupid and offensive.

Tosser	Self-flagellator and a show-off.
Fuck Stick	Clueless moron.
Ratbag	Maker of non-serious trouble.
Dick Head	Buffoon.
Suck Hole	Obsequious flatterer.
Dog	Snitch.
Standover Man	Bully.
If He Bought a Kangaroo, It Wouldn't Hop	Unlucky and not streetwise.
Pull Your Head In	Stop showing-off.
Pull Your Finger Out	Stop being lazy.

PISS

Piss is generally accepted as the act of urination. Australians have refined this essential human function into an array of emphatic statements that come in handy in any situation.

Piece of Piss	Easy.
Piss Off	Instructing someone to go away.
Piss On	To continue drinking.
Piss Up	Social gathering with the aim of getting drunk.

Piss Around	To dawdle.
Pissed	Drunk.
Pissed Off	Vexed.
Piss Easy	Task accomplished without trouble.
Piss Poor	Lame effort.
Piss Weak	Disappointing.
Piss Head	Serious drinker.
Piss Bolt	To achieve top speed while running away.
Piss Take	Sarcastic send-up.
To Piss in Someone's Pocket	To flatter someone's ego.

SHIT

First documented in the 1300s as one of the original four-letter Anglo-Saxon words, s-h-i-t is much more than a simple noun. Australian scholars have taken this most egalitarian of functions to its logical refinement. A variation for every situation.

Deadshit	A jerk.
Happy as a Pig in Shit	Having achieved a level of contentment contained in scripture.
Has Shit for Brains	Stupid.
Going Ape-shit	Extreme behaviour, usually anger.
Shit-a-brick	Exclamation of surprise.

Packing Shit	Declaration of fear.
Shithouse	No good.
Shitkicker	Lowest rung on the worksite.
Shit-stirrer	Troublemaker.
The Shit Hit the Fan	Trouble.
Bored Shitless	Very, very bored.
To Hang Shit	To taunt and ridicule.
Shit-faced	Completely drunk.
Shithead	Low intelligence/contemptible.
Shit Yourself	As stated.
Shit-list	Group of hated things.
Shit, Eh?	How about that?
Shit Can	Discard/dismiss/abandon.

FUCK

Fucker	General abuse to discredit a person or object.
Fuck Over	To cheat.
Fuck About	To waste time.
Fuck Around	To sleep around.
Fuck All	To do next to nothing.
Fuck With	To meddle.
Fucking Oath	Emphatic agreement.
Fuck's Sake	Statement of exasperation.
Fuck Me Dead	Astonishment (not to be taken literally).
Fucking Hell	Expressing surprise.
Fucked Up	Severe drug or alcohol impairment.
Fuckwit	Blanket term denoting unlikeable arsehole.
Fuckhead	Holder of indefensible views.
Fuck Load	A tremendous quantity.
I'm Not Here to Fuck Spiders!	I'm here to get the job done.

BASTARD

Bastard	Term of begrudging respect, 'You kissed Rita? You bastard.'/Low-level disrespect, 'Jimbo left before his shout, bastard.'
Old Bastard	Connotes age or length of association.
Useless Bastard	No respect meant.
Bloody Bastard	Disrespect meant.
Fucking Bastard	Denotes hatred.

ARSE

Arse	Short for arsehole.
Arsy	Lucky.
Arse About	Back-to-front.
Arse Up	Upside down.
Kiss My Arse	Not going to happen.
Arse like a Working Bullock	Fat-bottomed.
Arse about with Care	Mistake made because someone tried to assist.
Given the Arse	Sacked from work/relationship/team.
Down on His Arse	Tough life circumstance.

BLOW

Blow	Orgasm or cocaine.
Blow Job	Oral sex.
Blow Through	To leave.
Blow Shit out of Someone	Severe rebuke.
Blow In	Uninvited guest.
Blowie	Blowfly.
Blow a Fuse	Outburst of anger.
Blow Your Dough	To waste money.

THE LUCKY COUNTRY

You will often hear this phrase when Australians refer to their homeland. Given the number of poisonous animals, the distance from the rest of the world and the frequency of floods, fires and droughts, you may wonder why. But Australia's climate, stable political system, unique flora and fauna and abundant natural resources equate to a great quality of life.

COULD/COULDN'T

Could Sell You the Harbour Bridge
A skilled orator.

Could Sell Coal to Newcastle
A great salesperson (Newcastle is a prolific coal mining region).

Could Sell Ice to Eskimos
As above.

Could Kick the Arse off an Emu
Fast runner/rare good health.

Could Talk the Leg off a Horse
Loves a chat.

Could Talk under Wet Cement
Overenthusiastic orator.

Couldn't Run a Chook Raffle
Unskilled blunderer.

Couldn't Organise a Rock Fight in a Quarry
Incompetent.

Couldn't Organise a Piss-up in a Brewery
Unforgiveable ineptness.

Couldn't Organise a Root in a Brothel
Gross incompetence.

Couldn't Be Done in a Month of Sundays
Emphatic negation of statement.

Couldn't Drive Ducks to Water
Very poor driver.

Couldn't Drive a Nail into a Bucket of Water
Poor handyman.

Couldn't Fight His Way out of a Wet Paper Bag
Weakling.

Couldn't Pull the Skin off Custard
Physically weak and frail.

Couldn't Run a Bath
Sub-standard organisational skills.

Couldn't Give a Shit
Unconcerned with outcome.

Couldn't Find His Buttocks with Both Hands, a Roadmap and a Flashlight
Stupid.

Couldn't Hit the Side of a Barn
A bad shot.

Couldn't Organise a Fart in a Bean Factory
Simply no hope of a favourable outcome.

Couldn't Win Even if He Started the Night Before
Runner favoured to come last.

Couldn't Lie Straight in Bed
A liar.

'YEAH, NAH'

This often-heard phrase that can be confusing in the first instance. It means, 'Yes, I hear what you have said, but no, that is not the way I see it.' Essentially this is a phrase you would use to ignore someone's sage advice whilst giving the impression you have thoughtfully considered it. 'Yeah, nah' is further complicated by variations including:

'Nay, yeah'   Meaning yes.

'Nay, yeah nah'   Meaning no.

'Yeah, nay yeah'   Meaning yes.

YOU DON'T WANT TO BE KNOWN AS:

Gutless Wonder	A coward.
Dud Root	Bad at sex.
Goose	An idiot.
Drop Kick	A mindless fool.
Wearing of Brown Underpants	A weakling.
Beer Bottle	Empty from the neck up.
Pothole	Always in the road.
Showbag	Full of crap.
Dull as Dishwasher	Tedious and dull.
Crooked as a Dog's Hind Leg	Dishonest/liar.
Cunning as a Dunny Rat	Devious and sly.
Funny as a Fart in a Phone Box	Lacking a sense of humour.

TA FOR READING

You bloody beauty! Onya! If it was up to me, you would get a free tattoo of the Southern Cross on your buttock, a six pack of coldies, a surf lesson, a shark bite first-aid course ... or, you know, something dead-set useful.

Not to worry though.

In your travels, there is bound to come a time you will be left scratching your head over a fair dinkum conundrum. Drop a phrase in the local dialect and a couple of cobbers will appear to lend a hand.

**Don't be shy. Get out there and have a go.
It's another cracking day Down Under.**